Befo

We must first go over the basics about this book (I say *we* because you, the reader, are as much a part of this as I am). The reason I decided to write a poetry book is because it seemed as though everyone was writing a two-hundred-plus page book about what is wrong with their world or our world. That kind of book was my original intention, but then it struck me that, at times, those books can become redundant and or drawn out. Since not many people have been using poetry lately, I decided using my poetry was the way to go. In addition, with the use of my poetry, I can still express my feelings, but I can do it in a way that will be straight to the point and straight from the heart without trying to bullshit my way just to fill a certain amount of pages.

I think you'll find the way this poetry is written is unique in that it is quick, fast-paced, and has a different style to it. I would compare it to Russell Simmons' Def Poetry (if you haven't heard of it, check it out). It is also unconventional poetry for a book because it has more of a hip-hop flavor to it. Before you get all crazy and start saying things like, "Oh, he's just another white boy trying to rap and be black," understand it's not like that and that's not what I'm trying to be. I'm just being me and if you don't understand that right now, I suggest you go to Part III of this book and read "DiscrimiNation" before you read any further.

Anyway, they teach you in school to pause after every line when you read poetry; well, I don't want you to do that. If there is a comma at the end of the line you can pause, but if not, I want you to keep reading like it is all one sentence. Not every line is capitalized like traditional poetry either. The only time a new line starts with a capital letter is at the beginning of a new sentence, if the line starts with a name, or if I'm referring to myself in the first person. I thought about writing all the poems in paragraph form, but I found it was too hard to see which words were meant to rhyme. So I wrote with lines, so that while you read, you will be able to see the rhymes more easily. Another thing about the way this book is written is if you see that I've dropped the letter 'g' from an '-ing' word, for instance, I spell 'taking,' as 'takin,' then you should realize this is not because I don't know how to spell–it is purely done for stylistic reasons. How I spell a word is how I want that word to sound when you read it in your head, out loud, or however it is you read. Also, don't be shocked if you see a cuss word from time-to-time; there's already been one in this opening if you didn't notice. As a nineteen-year-old it's just the way I tend to talk and I see no harm in a cuss word every now and then and hopefully you won't have a problem with it either.

Now, the book is broken into four parts, some of which are broken down into two sub-sections. The content in these four parts are about the different aspects of what goes on in my mind and in my life. The four parts are based on the four subjects most mind-numbing in life– family, love/sexuality, problems in America and the world, and finding inspiration and a purpose in life.

Before each part I will give a brief introduction about the content of that particular portion of the book. Each part contains poems that flow into the next in order to tell a story, prove a point, and get a message through to you, the reader. Some poems are completely true to experiences I've had, some are things that didn't actually happen to me but to other people I know or are based on who I am, while others are based upon information I've learned and dis-

Poetry is Power

By

Ty Brack

Copyright ©2004 All Rights Reserved
ISBN 1-59405-060-0
Reproduction in any medium without written
consent of the author is expressly prohibited
Published by N2Print
Published and Printed in the United States of America

covered. All the poems are 100% true to who I am, how I feel, how I think, and what I believe.

All right, enough with the basics about the book, let's get down to the reason this book was written. First of all I want everyone to know this book is for anyone and everyone. Not only is this written to help keep my sanity, it is also written for you. It is written not only for my generation, but for the generations above, below, and yet to come. It is written with the vision that when you read this you will be able to relate in some form to what I have to say. It is written to inspire you to be able to find a way to express yourself. Perhaps after reading this, you will take up writing poems, or stories, or music. Perhaps just by reading this you will be able to share your emotions better with others. Even if just one simple idea strikes a chord with you, I will have done what I set out to do. After all, if more people could be able to express themselves and release all their bottled up emotions in ways such as music, speaking, talking to a loved one, or sharing information with and helping others, the world would be a much better place.

Speaking of the world being a better place that is another reason I wrote the book. A lot of you may be thinking, "Well why should I listen to a 19 year-old and why does he want to change the world?" Well, I'll tell you why. You should listen to what I have to say because there are very few, if any, 19 year-olds standing up for what they believe in right now. Because there are very few, if any, 19 year-olds making their voice heard. I want to change the world because I do not like the road we are heading down. Because I want a better world for my generation, for my children's generation, and for my grandchildren's generation. And I believe that the first step in my slight role to change the world is with this book. And the steps that follow will be continuing to express myself, my opinions, and my beliefs in a positive manner until the day I die and hopefully I will have sparked someone else along the way to do the same.

Now, we're sentences away from getting down and dirty, but there's one last thing before we get started and that is while you're reading, just remember to think in a different light than you ever have before. I want you to be able to relate in some way to what I have to say. I would like you to think about how you can use my words to your benefit, and I want to think about how you can use your *poetry as power*. What do I mean by that? Well keep reading and you'll find out. See, my poetry just happens to be poetry, and writing, and speaking, but yours may be something different. Like I said, keep reading, and you just may find out because…

Poetry is Power

Introduction Poem

My poetry began when I was 10 years old,
and it began the first time I spoke…

Thru My Microphone

Thru My Microphone,
I'ma make my way out this medium-sized home,
take ideas of those who inspire and mold em into my own.
I'ma transport my life into a brand new zone,
and accomplish everything I ever told my ex-girlfriend over the telephone.

Thru My Microphone,
I'ma establish myself in the business of broadcastin,
and assume the job of story tellin
durin important events,
mainly political or sportin,
creatin the images,
sendin em back to all you at home listenin.
But man,
that shit is just my in.

Cuz this is like some sort of sick addiction,
one taste of the mic sends me to a whole nother dimension.
That's why the switch of this mic tatted on my spine
will always be flipped in the on position.
That's why broadcastin won't be my story's end,
I got a helluva lot more to unload outta this mind

my friend.

Thru My Microphone,
I'ma teach myself to sing,
then jump in front of a camera and start acting.
Sing about shit that's real,
portray characters people can feel,
make a few mill,
but I won't let money be my Achilles heel.
Not gonna suffer from greed,
use enough dough to supply what I really need.
Then give the rest to my family,
and start a trustworthy charity.

Cuz this is like some sort of sick addiction,
one taste of the mic sends me to a whole nother
dimension.
That's why the switch of this mic tatted on my spine
will always be flipped in the on position.
That's why broadcastin, singin, and actin won't be my
story's end,
I got a helluva lot more to unload outta this mind
my friend.

And Thru My Microphone,
I'ma release all the pain and anger
that I've kept locked in a closet hangin on a hanger,
cuz that shit's reachin the point of danger.
I'ma help parents and children alike,
so they'll learn to cooperate and do what's right.
I'ma preach the importance of truth and love,
and pray for all the hate to be taken care of.
I'ma make my family finally understand

who I truly am.
I'ma make a difference in the life
of a person sufferin from strife.
I'ma stand up for my right to have an opinion,
and to choose just what it is I want to believe in.
I'ma express my concerns
for all the bullshit goin on in this world.
I'ma speak straight from the heart and the soul,
and in doing so,
achieve every single solitary goal.
But all that shit starts right here with my poetry
and this first poem.
And all that shit is gonna happen right here,
Thru My Microphone.

Part I

Family Matters

This first portion of the book is about me, and my family. And though I love them and they love me, for my entire life I've been looked at differently than anyone else in the family. This comes from people inside and outside as well, because as a member of this family you are expected to turn out a certain way. I do not dislike my family; I just dislike the way I am perceived because of my last name and the way my family thinks about what goes on within us and throughout the world.

We all love our families and we all have our problems with our families. This is just my way to release my anger, anxiety, or whatever you want to call it about issues inside my family. I'm not trying to run them down and I hope they don't take it that way. I hope you don't take it that way, either. I just want to make us a better family and I want to be truly understood by the people I love most.

Also, I know there are a lot of you out there who have far worse problems with their families than I. My parents aren't divorced, I am by no means living in poverty, but hopefully, all of you, no matter what social status you've been classified into, can find something you can relate to or find useful in making your family better as well. Remember, not only am I writing to express my feelings for the sake of my well-being, I'm writing for all of you and I'm using my poetry to do it.

Part I is dedicated to anyone who's having a hard time figuring out who they are because they're living their life based on what their family wants them to do, what they think their family wants them to do, or who they think they're supposed to be because of their family's history.

Let us all break loose.

Here we go…

Unleashing

Nearly twenty,
all these years I been buildin up plenty.
So I've decided it's time to let myself loose
from this noose
and share this shit with all yous.

At first glance I may come off as quiet and shy,
but if you get to know me,
I think you'll think I'ma pretty cool guy.
Oh yeah,
my real name's Ty,
but y'all can call me Fly.

Poetry is Power

Add a vek to the end and ya get Flyvek.
Now that's a name that's a nick,
or ya could say it's a nick that's a name.
There's yer basics,
now I'ma unclog the drain.

Ya see for what it's worth,
I been gifted with this curse
that since birth
has caused me to think too damn much,
so on the outside I may look tough,
but on the inside I been all messed up.

For nineteen years I been someone I'm not,
livin my life based upon what other people thought.
People inside and outside my family,
always tryin to be what they wanted me to be,
steada just bein me.
Always in my brother's shadow cuz he was the poster child.
A problem I shrugged off,
treated it so mild,
in reality that shit was deep down drivin me wild.

I wish I could go back to high school,
get a head start on the person I'm turnin into today,
rather than bein so caught up in an image I thought I had to portray.
Now I'm tryin to break away,
I'm tryin to become the person I was the whole entire way.
The person I didn't even know existed,
the person whose insides aren't so twisted.

I'm startin to find out as time passes we don't change ya see,
we just evolve into who we are meant to be.
But this evolution ain't easy,
especially when your family wants you to do things the way they see.
Especially when that family is mine,
and that family has a certain set of values expected of me.
That's why I always make sure I make them happy,
but I'm tired of doin things just to make them happy.
I'm tired of conformin to the rest of the family's beliefs.
So this is where I tell em how I really feel.
I'ma take my head out from under the sheets,
this is where the emotion gets unleashed.

Understand Me

Listen,
I'm not tryin to lay any blame,
but it's a cryin shame
that my mom is the only one who truly understands
what's goin on in my brain.

Ya see,
I'm an outcast cuz I think on a different level.
Plus I listen to rap, rock, and some of that Nu Metal.
And y'all just don't know what it's like to be a Brack,

stereotyped as a jock.
I forgot to tell ya that Brack,
is actually pronounced Brock,
that's why it rhymes with jock,
plus it's a name synonymous with jock.

Cuz as a Brack,
playin baseball is life.
For years I pretended to want that life,
live that life,
till I couldn't take that life,
so I quit that life,
but cuz I say announcin baseball will be my next life,
people are still prouda my life.

Yeah I love to announce,
that's right,
didn't I say I was addicted to the mic?
But the truth is that I wanna use the mic in other ways.
But I don't dare tell anyone that cuz I know I'll receive some sort of bullshit phrase,
"Well, Ty without sports how can you go about your days?"

Man,
it's so pathetic,
whenever I express myself outside of athletics,
it's like I'm not even present,
like I'm out from an anesthetic.

So what if I listen to Eminem?
I know criticizin my family may even sound a lil like

him,
but I had this shit figured out before I ever listened to
his big white mouth,
so don't blame him.
Everything inside my heart and mind is derived
from bein deprived
of bein recognized
by the people I hold closest in my life.

And love my family,
I do,
and I know they love me too,
but what's different to them,
is normal to me and you.
Maybe it's the generation gap,
but the gap's big enough an entire ocean could slip
through.

See,
I choose to use my imagination
that way I won't suffer from mind masturbation.
Yet some people like to call me lazy,
cuz my job is usin my creativity.
Whether they know it or not,
what they're doin is distancing themselves from me.
And I can tell,
they're distancing themselves from the rest of the
world as well.

Look,
usin your imagination and creativity is the key
to understanding everything that goes on round you
and settin yourself free,

but that's something they can't see very easily.
That's why the first step in understanding all that,
is beginning to understand me.

My Tattoos

I'm sure if you've got a tattoo or two,
you're gonna feel what I'm bout to spew.

My tattoos are cool,
well, I think so,
but in the eyes of some I'ma fool
for goin out and permanently puttin shit on my body
that's un-natural.

A tattoo is not a sin,
just a symbol of expression,
or of an important event a person's been in.

My tattoos go straight down my spine,
I already told ya bout the mic that's flipped on all the time.
I didn't tell ya that the mic goes through a number 5.
Beneath the mic and the 5,
there's a pencil curvin through a number 3,
and beneath them is a notepad in the middle of a 0.
I guess it's sumpin you kinda have to see to believe.

The 5 is my lucky number,
the 3 and the 0 make the number 30,
which is my second fav,

Ty Brack

put these numbers together as 5-30,
and ya get the date of my birthday.

The mic is for my announcin and speakin,
the pencil and notepad for my writin,
and combining the three,
my tattoos rep my poetry.

But some people see me now as a freak,
like a tattoo turns me into someone new.
Hey whoa,
whaddya know,
I'm still the same person,
just the version with a constant reminder
of who I am and what I'm gonna do.
I'ma probably end up gettin more too,
like when my children are born,
I'ma put their initials on my chest,
right over my heart,
on my left breast.

I just hope my tattoos will quit bein such a shock,
just cuz I'ma Brack.

A Brief Feeling

Damn,
it feels so good to talk bout this shit like I never done before.
At the same time,
I'm not sure I should keep writin on this line,
I don't wanna say anything that'll hurt my immediate kind.
All I'm tryin to do is make them think in a different light.
I hope they believe me when I say I'm not tryin to start a family fight.
All this is just the way I feel at writin time,
plus I'm tired of cryin myself to sleep at night,
so I gotta keep writin,
cuz this is like therapy for my heart, body, and mind.
I still gotta few more things to get off my chest,
two more family issues to address.
So to my fam,
don't get stressed,
I'm just searchin for a way for us to act our best.
And to all the rest,
here's some more of which you may be able to apply to your nest,
the Family Matters must go on,
I'm not done with this subject yet.

Ty Brack

The Evil Green

Here's a problem that's plagued my family forever,
one of which may not be resolved,
never.
Planted along the long winding road was a seed,
possibly of greed,
or maybe of need.
Had it been greed or need,
the evil green grew from that seed.
And no,
it wasn't weed.
I'm talkin bout the kind of green which measures how
well in life you succeed.

Basically,
a shitload of money was stumbled upon by someone
inside this family.
Since their stumbling,
what has followed is the rest of us mumbling,
"Why do they need all that dough,
give some to us,
it would only be generous of them ya know."
They do give though.
Of course it takes countless hours of convincing,
which just leaves me wincing.
Cuz if it takes countless hours to convince,
then takin the green just doesn't make sense.
If they can't find it in them to give in the first place,
then acceptin the green just worsens the case.
Damn,
why is this concept so hard for us to embrace?

Better be careful or the evil green will get you like it's
got us.
Let it consume and it can blind you from the obvious.
Careful or the evil green will take control.
If you let it,
it will take over your soul.

Now we've accepted green that's tainted.
If I told y'all the amount,
by now you'da fainted.
It wasn't given from the heart,
rather from beggin for it to be split among us in parts.
And by takin the green in parts,
it's gonna split us apart.
Once we're split apart,
well,
that has trouble written all over it from the start.
That'll just bring out the deepest and darkest.
Jealousy, envy, greed,
I can see all this happening.
God,
why did we ever have to go and start this?

So I pray,
I wish we could just put all the money away.
Let's just be happy for all we have today,
cuz we already have a helluva lot more than most
people in this world can say.
We can thank God for the brand new houses,
all the vacations,
and all the shit we have we don't need.
Then move on with our lives,

chill out,
and forget the evil green ever took over this family.
Hell,
I've taken the evil green as well,
I'ma probably end up seein Satan anyway,
so what the hell else is there left to say,
other than…

Better be careful or the evil green will get you like it's got us.
Let it consume and it can blind you from the obvious.
Careful or the evil green will take control.
If you let it,
it will take over your soul.
I'm beggin you please,
don't let the evil green do what it's set out to achieve.

Uncle Rog

My Uncle Rog died around the age of fifty-five.
He wasn't married,
never had children,
but had an interesting life.
About the time he hit twenty,
he began educatin himself intently.
Read countless books,
got his degree,
then eventually landed a job that paid quite fully.

Somewhere down the line,
Rog's life got split in two different kinds.
People on the outside were always sayin,
"Gee, what a great guy!"
Meanwhile,
on the inside,
we couldn't figure out why.
Our vision of him was that of a hateful man,
who was always goin in the opposite direction of the family plan.
And though he did treat us poorly all the way through,
we honored his differing points of view
with a great big fuck you.
So as the years grew,
so too did the family feud.

There was constant behind the back talking,
along with backstabbing and name calling,
for that,
into hell we're probably all gonna be falling.

And to this problem there was no hope of ever resolving.

Uncle Rog died on that tenth day of July,
many of us didn't hold enough empathy for him to even cry.
After his death,
he is remembered as angry and mean,
but that doesn't stop us from wantin a slice of his evil green.
A member of this family is dead,
yet all we do is glare with eye's painted the devil's red.
All we do is plead
for a piece of his self-made fortune with hearts of greed.
If we could just take a step back into reality,
think to ourselves how he treated us and we treated he,
then it's pretty fuckin plain to see,
that shit doesn't belong to any of us,
we don't deserve none of that money.

And to think,
where did this all stem?
Simply cuz he had different ideas and we didn't even try to understand them.
So this is where our lives cross,
me and him.
Cuz my life is startin to look somewhat similar,
I'm startin to see things that to my family don't look so familiar.
My ideas are beginnin to be shut-down or debated,

which leaves me so fuckin frustrated.
They just don't get it.
This is how the conflict with Rog was originally created.
That is why this story was just told,
cuz I can see us startin to go down that same road.
Life is about ready to repeat.
And if we let it,
for the second time we will suffer defeat.

Now,
I'm just givin a heads up.
I've said all I need to say about my family matters so to this subject I'ma shut up.
With the use of my poetry it's onto Part II,
so I'ma turn the page,
and hope we can keep this conflict from again bein released outta the cage.

Part II

The Cycle of Love and Exploration of Sexuality

Part II is broken into two sections. **Section A** is about being in love for the first time as a young adult, the cycle in which that love takes place, and the stages in which the cycle of love consists. The initial feelings, the blossoming of the love, the realization of falling in love too deep, the feelings that are hurt after breaking up in a way never imagined, and the lessons learned from that first loving relationship.

Section B is about the exploration of sexuality and how the male's sexual mind is in a constant battle with their common sense. This section of **Part II** will also address the struggle to find one's sexual safe places; the struggle of exploring sexuality as a young adult, and the effects these experiences has on one's self. The content of the section is inspired partly from my experiences and partly from my beliefs about this subject. So some of it didn't actually happen to me and the time frame within the section is falsified, but it is what I think would happen should I choose to live that way.

The content in both sections can also at times get somewhat graphic, so be heads up. Hopefully, if you're usually offended by content like this, you'll be able to look past it and see the message I'm getting across with my poetry. Remember to be thinking about how you can use what I have to say in your poetry.

Part II is dedicated to anyone who's been through a weird and rough relationship or is struggling with how to handle their sexuality.

All that being said, let's talk about love and sex. Sound like fun? Of course it does.

Here we go again…

Section A

The Cycle of Love

Stage One

What Is This?

What is this feeling in my chest?
This girl makes me think I'm going into cardiac arrest.
I really hope this whole thing pans out.
God knows I wanna girlfriend to care about.
Yeah,
I'm only sixteen,
but this young lady makes me dream.
Looking at her picture sends me to a place peaceful and
serene.

What is this relationship?
It's beginning to feel like more than an innocent friendship.
I'd like to become more serious.
Not being around her leaves me lonely and furious.
In addition to the fact I'm young and curious.

What is this kiss?

That was the first time I ever touched those lips.
Still,
something feels amiss.
Are we together now?
Did it all begin with that kiss?
Even if it has begun,
I'll most likely only last a few months at the top of her list.
But am I even at the top of the list to begin with?
So again I ask,
What is this relationship?

A few months later...

Stage Two

Three Words

"I love you."
Phew.
Wait a minute,
what did I just do?
This relationship wasn't supposed to last.
It's been a couple of months and I love her,
is that too fast?
I don't care cuz this girl is simply amazin.
I'ma make those three words a regular occasion.
I can't get enough of her kiss,
the same one that sparked all this.
When we touch lips,

into a coma I slip,
nothing else matters when I'm locked in her grip.
And this whole thing is such a trip,
that's why I used those three words,
if I didn't I was gonna to flip.

Okay,
wake up,
I spaced out.
How long was my mind wandering about?
I hope she's not scared from the three words I just used.
I can't believe I just said *I love you*.
But now what is she gonna do?
"Ty *I love you* too."

Hell yeah!
I got the "I love you" return.
This is something new,
but I do have a few points of concern.
Where does it all go from here?
How does the fire stay warm enough to burn?
Is this love true?
Will it continue to churn?
I guess these are all things I'll just have to wait to learn.
For now,
I'm not gonna worry.
I'm just gonna bask in the glory
of what was said from me to her and her to me.
All it took were those three words,
that one simple line.
So many thoughts runnin through my mind,

I'm lettin myself fall in love for the first time.
A year later…

*** Stage Three ***

Too Deep

Comin up on our year and a half anniversary.
I'm bout to head off to a college or university.
She still has a year left in high school.
Man,
this decision's gonna be so cruel.
We already tried breakin up twice before,
but we just ended up wantin more.
Her and I can't get enough of each other's bodies.
We do engage in a number of sexual activities,
yet intercourse is one of our sexual oddities.
Makin love is a long way down our schedule,
that's part of what has made us so special.
Plus I get lost in her eyes,
and I love massagin those baby soft thighs.
I've become her hero and she's become mine,
I gotta be with this girl all the time.

Something tells me our relationship is becomin unhealthy,
leadin us down a path not so wealthy.
I'm afraid I might lose her,
cuz everything is startin to confuse her.
We're too young to be so perfect for each other.

We're too young to be clinging so tight to one another.
She's my best friend,
I want her till the end,
however,
I'm not so sure she sees it happenin.

How can this be fixed?
We're afraid to talk about the world outside us,
so time just ticks.
Pretty soon the problem won't be worth avoiding,
both of us are gonna be left hurt and voiding.
I just have this feeling we won't be able to stay together forever.
The day is nearing where we won't be able to be together whenever.
We shoulda stayed apart when we tried before.
We've sunken too deep into love's ocean,
too far from the surface and the shore.

And I've fallen even deeper than her.
I've let my love for her put me into a sleeper.
I know everything's not okay,
but I'm gonna keep lettin it go on with each day.
The relationship is in her hands,
it's up to her to make the play.

Half a year later...

Stage Four

I Never Thought

I knew the chance of us coming to a complete end existed,
but I never thought it would end the way it just did.
This shit is so twisted
the actions of which your betrayal consisted.
First of all,
I know we're on a break n all,
but you're still livin in my house
sleepin in my bed while I'm off at college,
but that's not all.
My parents are taking care of you,
cuz yours don't know how to take care of you.
And with all I've done for you,
with all the times you said *I love you*,
with how well I thought I knew you,
what you've done just couldn't have come from you.

I never thought you'd be the kind to go behind my back.
I just can't believe two people so good together could come to an end like that.

Okay,
the way this all went down doesn't sound so great,
so let me try and get all this straight.
You've gone to parties,
made out with guys numbering eight.
One of whom

took you into a separate room
and did stuff with you
I never even got to do.
Meanwhile I'm worryin about my first fall term,
listenin to you on the phone sayin you can't wait for my return,
but yer really out gettin a piece from some fuckin lil worm!
Sure you've told me the truth the now,
but the real truth is that you been lyin to me for months, wow.

I never thought you'd be the kind to litter our relationship with lies.
I just can't believe I'm seein this happen through my eyes.

Aight,
the more I sit here and think about it,
the more I sit here and get pissed about it.
I think I'm startin to flip out.
Why don't you get the fuck outta my house?
You've used me and my family.
All I ever did was love you
and my family provided you with hospitality.
And this is how you repay me?
So what if you still have your virginity.
I could care less now if you've never been fucked.
Because of this,
all my trust in you has been plucked.
In my mind yer just like every other bitch.
Yer no longer the girl I fell in love with.
And now you've destroyed us.

All the time we spent together,
our dreams of lasting forever,
everything's been crushed.

I never thought our relationship would end with me
bein so pissed.
I just can't believe you gave me a reason to think
about you like this.

Okay,
none of this was ever said to her face.
Right now I'm in my room trashin the fuckin place.
And I've fallen on my knees,
I'm beggin you God please,
tell me that didn't really happen,
tell me that shit was a tease.
I know God,
it wasn't a dream,
that's why I've begun to yell and scream.
That's why the tears are flowin down in a steady
stream.
I coulda gone off but I'm glad I kept it all in.
I'm glad I just released it all through this pen.
My love for her is too deep to act in opposition.
So I acted like I understood her position.
Nothin will ever be the same,
the way I look at her is gonna drastically change.

I never thought she would do something so fucked up.
I just can't believe how much repairin all this damage
is gonna suck.

    In the months following the breakup...

Stage Five

Lessons Learned

What happened still seems fucked up.
My insides are still all cut up.
I think I'm ready to talk to her again.
My love is too strong to never speak to her again.
We've got to figure out a way to put this behind.
Problem is,
it's always gonna be in backa my mind.

Why did she go and do what she went and did?
Sure,
I was always there,
but that instilled in her a frightening scare,
after all she's still just kid.
I smothered the girl,
I put too much pressure into just one whirl.
I already had us married with three children,
livin in a luxurious New York buildin.
She felt trapped.
And I never ever considered that.

It's all startin to ring true.
It wasn't all her fault,
it was mine too.
This was just her way of puttin it all to a halt.
It was a messed up way,
but now I understand it as I sit here and write this today.
This was just one of those weird life lessons.

At the time it hurts,
but it turns out to be one of life's blessins.

Thanks to her I realize I've got the rest of my life
to go out and find the woman meant to be my wife.
There are way too many people in this world
to narrow it down to the first and only girl.
I'ma get up,
get out,
and get some experience.
Get around and provide myself with some variance.

Oh yeah,
I'm happy to report I've made up with my first love.
Our relationship has finally come to a healthy end.
We've become each other's best friend.
So now,
I'm ready to live my life single and free.
Hey,
it's time to explore my sexuality.

Section B

Exploration of Sexuality

Operation Exploration

Mr. Flyvek,

You are now free of any commitment to the opposite sex. It is now time for you to explore your sexuality freely and become special agent Flyvek. Let this 1st day of January, year 2004, be declared the starting point for classified top secret, Operation Flyvek-530, otherwise known as Operation Exploration.

Operation Objectives:

1.) Explore the female body and let the female body explore you.
2.) Explore as many female bodies as possible and let your body be explored as much as possible.
3.) Provide yourself with valuable sexual experience.

Operation Health and Emotional Safety Guidelines:

1.) Do not have sexual intercourse unless you feel she's right one. (You are not a man-whore)
2.) If you do have sexual intercourse, use a prophylactic. (You are not going to get any STD's – that would be a failure)
3.) Do not do anything that will violate yourself or a person of the opposite sex. (You don't want to end up in jail)

Operation Advice:

1.) In the heat of battle, think with your big head, not your little head.
2.) Don't think about your first love while performing an operation. (Doing so could ultimately destroy the operation)
3.) Be *you*, have fun, but be smart as well.

Okay, special agent Flyvek, everything's laid out for you. Now get out in the world and explore. You have the eight months you have left this year at college to complete this assignment. You must follow your operation objectives, health and safety guidelines, and please, use the advice. You must accomplish as much as you can, anything less is unacceptable.

Do you accept this mission? Let us know.

RE: Operation Exploration
To whomever it may concern,

I do accept this mission. I will do my best to fulfill the objectives of the "Operation," and I will do my best to follow the health and safety guidelines as well as the advice. I am extremely eager to begin exploring my sexuality, so I will not waste any more time writing this return letter. Operation Exploration begins tonight.

Sincerely,
Special Agent Flyvek

The Operation Begins

Okay,
here I go,
let the operation begin.
I'm chillin in my lazy-boy with my hand rubbin my chin.

I'm checkin out the scene,
and to be honest I'm likin what I'm seein.
Especially this one chic.
blonde,
long legs,
extra thick.
I take another alcohol sip
and hope she ain't a trick.

The alcohol kicks in,
completin the conversion
from my personality's introversion
to my personality's extroversion.

Now we're hittin it off,
I'm on a roll,
whisperin in her ear real soft.
I can feel a positive vibe,
so I invite her up to my room to be alone
and get away from the downstairs tribe.

We're on my bed,
her on her back,
and me lookin in her eyes.

My fingers tickle her forehead,
the music on just a crack,
then suddenly a dilemma begins to arise...

The Brain versus The Penis

Ah great,
why does this have to happen?
I thought I drank enough alcohol to keep you strapped in.

Nope,
I'm back and ready to check things out.
Just keep kissin her,
it keeps the blood flowin about.

Ya know this is my first time with this girl?

Of course I do,
it's my first time with her too.
That's why I woke up so fast,
plus she's got an unbelievable ass.

So you probably want me to take advantage of this girl?

Naturally,
that's the other reason I woke up so fast.
Why don't you slide your hand over her ass?

Good idea,
no wait,
I'm not lettin you win tonight.

Poetry is Power

I'm just makin out,
that's all,
aight?

                                            Yeah,
                                             well,
                                        we'll see.
                              You may think you can,
                              but you can't control me.

Listen,
she's just a confidence builder.
Now why don't you go away cuz you ain't gettin in
her.

                                    Just keep on kissin,
                                      slip her the tongue,
                                         grab that ass,
                                    unbutton them pants,
                       show her how well you're hung.

Mmm,
her ass is perfect,
her tongue's movin in waves.
I'll unbutton them pants,
wait a sec,
I gotta behave.
No more listening to you,
shrivel back down in your cave.

                                               Jeez,
                                  don't be so harsh.
                                      C'mon Fly,
                                    have some fun.

> She's likes it,
> it's not like she's a nun.

That doesn't matter.
There's lots of operations left,
she's just the first step to the ladder.
Goin any further would be a theft.

> Oh will you stop!
> Listen to yourself,
> *a theft?*
> Her cherry's already gone pop.
> Just quit thinkin and let me get wet.

Aight,
that's it,
I've heard enough.
You think just cuz you're erect you're tough.
I'ma take the Operation's advice,
big head over little head,
I don't need your perverted advice.

> You can't get rid of me Fly.
> You gotta use me while you can,
> I'm reachin my sexual prime.
> You know you wanna hear this girl moan and whine.

I said that's it!
I don't need your shit.
I can get rid of you just watch.
"Baby,
I think we need to tone this down a notch."

Poetry is Power

            Whoa,
       what the hell you doin?
         Don't say that,
this whole thing is gonna be ruined.
             Man,
     I was on the verge of screwin.

"Right now we're movin at the speed of light,
so I think we should just call it a night."

          You son of a bitch!
        There goes the blood flow.
             Man,
         you really do blow.

Told ya I'm stronger.
Like I said,
we got lots of time,
just wait a lil longer.
The way you were thinkin tonight,
man,
we woulda committed a crime.

            Yeah, whatever,
     I can't comprehend what you're tellin me.
     All I heard was something bout a felony.
            I'm too weak,
        no more actin like a pimp.
        I'm officially goin limp.

You know I'm waitin for the one that's right?
And that wasn't the one tonight.

Understand I can't do all the explorin in just one
night.

>   Uh huh,
>   whatever.
>   You're so clever.
>   I envy you Fly.
>   I'ma bout to say *goodbye*.

I'm sorry I hurt your feelings.
Don't worry,
I'ma make it up to ya in the mornin with a lil hand
healing.

>   Well that's the least you could do.
>   Thanks so much dude.

This was good cuz now we know who rules who.
The rest of this operation will go smooth,
cuz I can overpower you.
I didn't think it was possible,
but now I'm in complete control.

> In the months following…

Movin Forward

(The names given in this poem are fictional)

Now that I know my penis doesn't control my brain,
but rather my brain controls my penis,
I can push forward the train toward a successful
operation which won't do anything to demean us,
that is,
my brain and my penis.

The exploration keeps marchin on,
and without even havin to put a condom on,
I'm findin out a lot about myself and what turns me on.

A chick with thick full hair,
who walks round without a care,
knows what to wear,
can stop you dead in your tracks with one glamorous glare,
is confident in what she has,
and isn't afraid to rock it with a stylistic flare.

A girl who can harness her sexual energy till we,
get alone in a room
where she releases it all with a boom
and we,
make up a kinky scenario,
all while softly playin some Norah Jones over the stereo.
All while lookin each other square in the eyes,

playin with our bodies
till the morning sunrise.

All that up there forms the prototype.
How am I gonna find someone who lives up to all that hype?
That list was put together thanks to the experience attained so far durin this Exploration.
Not one girl had all those things built up in their reputation.
Each girl was lucky to hold just one
and that's how I figured out the kinda girl I want.

From Teri to Keri,
Amanda to Samantha,
Sarah and Tara,
they all played an important role,
but I'm findin myself wantin to put the Operation on hold.
There's still a lotta time left though,
at the same time this whole thing is gettin old.
Inside I'm startin to feel lonely and cold.
Maybe I should just quit and lay low for awhile,
or I could keep movin forward and continue feelin like a pile
for bein with a different girl all the time
and puttin on this fake smile.

I guess that's what I'll do.
After all,
the operation said to get as much experience as possible,
I just have this feelin I'ma end up even more

frustrated,
but I'ma keep on gettin educated,
but man,
I'm wonderin what the hell I've created?

A few more months later…

Frustrations

Aight, that's it,
I've had it with this shit.
I'm tired of livin like this,
I quit.

I don't even give any of these girls a chance.
I just fool round with em and send em back into the dance.
How am I sposed to find the right one by goin bout it like that?
Maybe the goal of the operation is where I drifted off track.
"You must accomplish as much as you can.
Anything less is unacceptable."
But I have accomplished as much as possible and that's what I find unacceptable.
This shouldn't be how I have to get girls,
gettin drunk,
goin to parties with the world movin in swirls.
The person these girls are seein ain't the real Flyvek,

it's just another guy who thinks with his dick,
which I thought I had conquered cuz I never had sex
durin the Exploration.
But what I did do was just as bad and still resulted
from penis instigation.

Yeah I'm glad I got this experience,
however,
bein involved in this experiment
just created an interference in the rest of my life
and my independence.
An independence while I'm still young I should
cherish.
An independence that even when I find the one I
shouldn't let perish.

So ladies,
for the next several years I'ma lay low and just be me
and work on the person I need to be.
If you see me on the street and you like what you see,
you're welcome to give it a shot,
but most likely I won't be of any good to you
and we're both better off for now bein free.

Once again I've learned another one of life's lessons,
from a crazy experience that turns out to be one of
life's blessins.
I've done my exploring of sexuality,
I found out what I want and the kinda girl I need.
It's time for me to move away and start another day.
A day that leads to the rest of my existence,
now I can say this Operation Exploration is no longer
in existence.

Operation Exploration: Aborted

To whomever it may concern,

This day May 30, 2004, shall mark the end of classified top-secret, Operation Flyvek-530, otherwise known as Operation Exploration.

General Operation Information:

I explored the female body and let the female body explore me as much as possible. Yes, the sexual experience I provided myself with, though I am not proud of it all, is valuable because I learned from everything I did.

I did not become a man-whore, as I did not even have sexual intercourse with one female throughout the Operation because I did not find the right one. The right one is someone I will find when I am not looking to find them and when I am not performing an Operation such as this.

I am happy to report I did not receive any sexually transmitted diseases and did not even have to use a prophylactic. Although, I probably should have used one when I got oral from that one girl, she was real questionable. Anyway, I did not end up in jail either as I did not violate the beliefs of any of my female counterparts. However, I did violate myself at times.

Though I did not have sex, I still thought with my

little head, but still tried to convince myself I was not. I did not think about my first love while performing in the Operation, except now that it's over, she is still better than any girl I experienced in the duration of the mission. That fact is going to be a conflict in the future as she went through the same Operation, but found someone and was able to move on from me. Meanwhile, I went through my Operation and did not find someone new, but instead I fell in love with my first love even more. That is something I will have to overcome in the days ahead.

In Conclusion:

Ultimately, it came down to the fact that I was quickly becoming someone I did not want to become. I was having too much fun and not being as smart as I should have been. That is why I, Special gent Flyvek, wish to resign from classified top-secret Operation Flyvek-530, otherwise known as Operation Exploration. Thank you for the opportunity and I learned a lot about myself during my time spent on this mission. But, with your permission, I would like to return to my normal civilian life so I can concentrate on more important things, such as fighting for our rights and for peace.

Sincerely,

Former Special Agent Flyvek

RE: Operation Exploration: Aborted

Mr. Flyvek,

Permission to return to your normal civilian life has been granted. We would have liked to see you battle through and make it the full eight months, but we understand you have more important life issues you want to fight. Good luck with your future, and we expect to see you back exploring your sexuality again someday.

Sincerely,

Whomever it Concerned

Halfway Mark

Well, we've hit the halfway mark. Take a break, put the book down for a sec, grab something to eat, call your mom, call your girlfriend or boyfriend, call someone you haven't spoke with in a long time. Tell them something you've never told them or anyone else before. Clear up a dispute you had, or simply tell them you love them. That's what I just did with the first two parts of the book, and hopefully you could relate to my poetry and hopefully it will help you in some way. Hey, what the hell ya still reading for? Go talk to somebody.

Oh, you're back. So did you do it? Good. Now, let's get ready for the second half of the book. The final two parts of the book are not as extremely personal as the first two. Yes, they are personal in the sense that what I write is what I believe, but the issues I will discuss from here on out are more global, more outside of myself and my immediate surroundings.

Once again, the purpose is that hopefully you'll be able to take something out of what I have to say, apply it to your life, and think about things more or in a different light than you did before. (Hah, I rhyme even when I'm not trying to). If you're on the same side of the fence as me on some of the issues coming up then you'll be able to relate. If you're not on the same side of the fence then hopefully you'll gain a greater understanding and respect for the other side. Remember to be thinking about how you can use your poetry. If you haven't figured out what I'm talking bout, just keep reading my poetry, you'll figure it out soon enough. Ya ready? I am.

Follow me...

Part III

The Fights for what's Right

Like **Part II**, **Part III** will be separated into two sections, which are actually two different fights. Not fights with fists, or guns, or bombs, but with words. And they are meaningful fights. Fights that many people have fought before and will continue to.

Fight #1 is the fight to stop hate toward homosexuality, different races, and religion. *Fight #2* deals with more political type issues inside our government, our people, and throughout the world. It is a fight to express concerns for America and the world without being called a traitor, and with the purpose of making people understand what it means to be American and how America can get better than it already is, or isn't.

Part III is dedicated to all those striving for free-minds, free-hearts, and freedom. It is dedicated to those who are looking for a way to better their world and our world.

In order to get **Part III** under way, let me explain that the main, overriding message of **Part III**, lies within my poetry and...

Ty Brack

The First Amendment

December 15, 1791,

The First Amendment, created with the help of Founding Fathers such as James Madison and Thomas Jefferson, is ratified into the Constitution of the United States of America. The Amendment states...

Congress shall make no law respecting an establishment of religion, or prohibiting the free exercise thereof; or abridging the freedom of speech, or of the press; or the right of the people peaceably to assemble, and to petition the government for a redress of grievances.

This means I have the right to say everything I already have and everything I am about ready to. This also means you have the right to agree, disagree, or dispute what I have already said and what I am about to. I have no problem with that, but I do have a problem with the fact that the First Amendment is continually ripped away from the people without the people even knowing it. I have a problem with all the books, music, television shows, and movies which have been and still are being banned, restricted, or censored by the government all for fear of offending certain groups of people. When in fact these books, music, television shows, and movies actual speak the truth and have the right to be made the way they were originally intended. That right is given in the First Amendment.

I have a problem with the people who believe the First Amendment was written with Christianity and only Christianity in mind because Madison and Jefferson were themselves Christian. When in fact, they designed the First Amendment on the basis that anyone is free to join any kind of religion.

I have a problem with the people who abuse The First Amendment by saying, writing, or gathering in ways that lack common sense and promote hateful causes. Though Madison and Jefferson meant for all kinds of speech to be protected whether they be hateful or peaceful, you would think we would have learned by now that hate breeds murder, rape, and war. Hate breeds our slow demonic demise.

Why is a 19-year-old fighting these people? Because it is my patriotic duty as an American to stand up and fight for a better way of life. It's your patriotic duty as well.

And what can I do about all this? What can we do about all this? Well, the best way to counter these problems is to fight back with our rights that are guaranteed to us in the First Amendment. And that's what I intend to do. I am not going to counter hate with hate. Instead I am going to counter hate with the promotion of love, with the promotion of open-mindedness, peace, freedom, and acceptance for all. I'm going to counter the violations of our rights in the First Amendment by exposing those violations and expressing my own beliefs and concerns for our people, our nation, and our world. I'm going to do this with the help of my poetry and knowledge I've given to myself and others have given to me about the subjects

I will discuss.

If you don't like what I have to say then you can counter me. If you are a hateful person, you can continue to express your hate because you have that right. But if you feel the same way I do, then you have the right to say what you want to say and you should stand up and say it. And eventually enough people who love their country, who pray for peace and love, who are open-minded, and who want to make a difference will speak out and fight. And eventually we will all be able to make that difference, and make that change, and continue to push the human race onward and upward to limits never imagined.

Now is the time to use my poetry, to use our poetry to stand and fight for our rights to the freedoms of speech. Now is the time to stop the censorship of the truth. Now is the time to stop the hate. Now is the time to set the record straight with all generations of Americans. Now is the time to open all our minds and finally come together as "one nation under god, indivisible, with liberty, and justice for all."

Fight #1

*Stopping the Hate:
Peace, Freedom, Acceptance, and
Love for All*

The first thing we must know to start this fight, is we must know exactly...

What Hate Is

Hate is outdated.
Hate is useless.
Hate is disrespectful.
Hate is close-mindedness.
Hate is discrimination.
Hate is racism.
Hate is rape.
Hate is raping all who strive for peace.
Hate is the root of all that is evil.
Hate is creating a world that is scaring my future wife and unborn children.
Hate is a force that separates good and innocent people without reason.
Hate is destruction.
Hate must be destroyed before it destroys us.

Right now ya may be wandering,
"How do we open our minds and accept?
How do we stop hating?"
Well it all starts by not being...

Brainwashed

People keep telling me that because I've changed my views and beliefs since entering college that I've been brainwashed. They say I've been brainwashed by the music I listen to or the books I read. However, in reality, I'm opening my door and letting in all types of information, absorbing it all, then forming my own thoughts and breaking away from the crowd. Those of us who choose to educate ourselves about what goes on around us are actually broadening our horizons and learning to accept ideas that are thought to be wrong, but aren't really all that wrong.
We are not being brainwashed.

Let me explain what being brainwashed is...

To the kids,
If you allow yourselves to be taken in by a group just cuz you want to fit in,
even though being in that group isn't being true to what's deep down within you,
and you start treating other kids like trash just so you can get the image of a bad ass,
you're letting yourselves be brainwashed.

To the parents,
If you don't teach yourselves about sex, music, and drugs,
how can you teach your children about sex, music, and drugs?
Sit down and watch MTV with your son or daughter,

explain to them what's real and what's fodder,
that way we won't end up with another school slaughter.
But if you choose not to educate your children about a certain touchy subject,
cuz you think you're protecting them,
you're not.
You're just making them a subject to being brainwashed.

To everyone,
If you sit at home and believe everything you see on TV,
or if you never think about questioning authority.
If you suffer from cognitive dissonance,
in other words you suffer from ignorance
cuz you only search for info to back beliefs belongin to your existence.
If you suffer from this then you will never accept an idea that's different than you.
Like a Caucasian,
who doesn't accept another race living in their location.
Or a devout Christian,
who won't tolerate other forms of religion.
Or a heterosexual,
who can't accept a homosexual.
If you can't accept,
if your door is locked,
you're brainwashing yourself.
And that's not good for your health.
Trust me,
I was brainwashed once myself,

until I opened my mind and stopped bein ignorant.
When you can do that you can become independent,
yet can still acquire love for everyone.
Once you stop bein brainwashed,
we can put an end to all the hate and discrimination.

Homophobic World

Welcome to the not so wonderful wide world of homophobia,
where people's actions are a bunch of bolognia.
Where the measure of a man is constructed through how many women he has slept with.
Where at the same time a woman is called a slut because of how many men she has slept with.
Where the thought of two people of the same sex holding hands is looked down upon,
spit upon,
and shit upon.
Where the sight of a man and another man holdin each other isn't seen as a part of God's plan.
Where those who are brave enough to come clean,
are cast out by certain people as part of Satan's team.

Where,
well,
by now ya get the picture.
Hatred toward homosexuality is still a formidable fixture.
Remember Matthew Shepherd.

Ty Brack

Brutally murdered
just cuz he chose to live his life under that word.

It's time to stop this nonsense.
It's time to use our common sense.
For crying out loud,
can't we see these people are proud?
Can't we see there isn't anything wrong with homosexuality?
Do we have to crucify them for what they do in privacy?
And I can't stand using the words them, they, or their.
Cuz it makes it sound like I don't care.
But I do care,
it's just the only way I can get my point across.
It's the only way I can express concern for all those being strapped to a cross.

And for what?
They still find love.
Just cuz they find love within the same sex,
they get an X marked on their chests.
They find love just like I find love for a female.
They find love just like a female finds love for me.
The way we treat homosexuality is gettin to be so stale.
Unfortunately this kind of hate and discrimination
isn't the only kind still tippin the scale...

DiscrimiNation

If this offends you then here's some tissues,
racism is still one of our nation's biggest issues.
Our nation is still better known as a DiscrimiNation.
Mainly cuz some of us are still thinking the white way.
I'm here to remind us that this isn't always the right way.

Under that way,
the freedom America was founded upon,
only applies to those who live in the light-skinned kingdom.
Once a person crosses over from the opposite side of the border,
they're immediately forced to conform to White American culture.
And if they embrace,
we let them call America their permanent resting place.
But if they don't embrace,
we label them a disgrace.

Like if people speak in a different dialect,
one that goes against the one the majority's picked,
they're immediately thought of as havin no intellect,
when really that's just the way they been raised,
but the majority hears the way they speak and gets crazed.

Or if a young white kid wants to start rhymin,

people will ask him,
"What you have you been smokin?
Jeez Fly,
yer so high yer flyin."
The answer to that question is I don't smoke,
and that question is such a joke.
Just cuz I write rhymes that may fall under Rap,
doesn't mean I'm tryin to be black.
It doesn't mean I don't wanna be white,
it's just the way I'm expressin myself aight.

Okay now,
dialect ain't the only thing this DiscrimiNation's made whack.
We all need to take a sec and look back,
we all need to remember how we been stagin an attack,
on people whom we label red, brown, yellow, and black.
We came from Europe and stole this land,
from the Native Americans and the Hispanics.
What followed were years of hateful tactics.
We enslaved the people who rightfully deserved to inhabit,
along with the others who longed for freedom and for a chance to grab it.

Flashback to present day,
slavery ended not too long ago in years goin the other way.
Or has it ended?
We still hire migrants on farms for way less than minimum wage pay.
So in a way,

we really haven't come a very long way.
People come to America lookin for that freedom they
keep hearin about,
but all they get is screwed and a,
"You're not American, get out!"

Sure you could argue
that the DiscrimiNation works in both directions,
with all the benefits given to those of a different
ethnical background.
But I say they deserve the benefits for all the years we
worked em into the ground.

Still when it comes right down to it,
we all need to say screw it.
We can remember the gruesome past,
we can take the way we still act today,
and make it the past,
and leave it all as just that,
the past.

Let's just realize
America is a place that's been formed on ideas taken
from all walks of creation.
That's why America doesn't belong to just us
Caucasians,
but to everyone.
So let's put an end to the hate,
and get rid of this DiscrimiNation.

But while we rid of the DiscrimiNation,
there's still another form of hate we're facin.
One of which adds to the DiscrimiNation's ongoin

complication,
and one of which plagues us just as well as every other nation…

The Big One

So we got Christians sayin they're the only way,
that's the way they're thinkin.
Meanwhile the Mormons are goin on their missions,
gettin dissed on by Catholics who don't support their positions.
Those within Judaism disagree with those who are Catholic.
And Judaism is misunderstood by those who believe in all things Islamic.

So ya see this is the big one,
this constant debate over religion.
A debate that often leads to hate,
a hate that often leads to war,
a war with no solution in store.
Like the one in the Middle East
that's been goin on for 10,000 years at least.
That's why I know,
this may be one of the many fights that can't be won.
But if these fights are gonna be won,
they have to start somewhere,
so why can't I be the one?

People keep raisin the question,
"Is Jesus Christ white or is he black?"
That sounds like a racist issue,
that's where that question takes us back.
Or how bout this question,
"Does God accept homosexuality or doesn't he?"
Well that one takes us back to our world of

homophobia,
gee.

Now doesn't it seem,
all this bickering over which religion is the correct team
creates more hate than the Supreme Being could ever dream?
I say the Supreme Being because I believe.
Cept I don't label this Being a he or a she.
Nor do I associate this Being with a face or a race.
I just believe this Being is there for all of us,
and can take any shape or form,
so there's no need for such a shit storm.
No matter if you believe in Jesus,
Jehovah,
Buddha,
or Allah,
just know there is that one Force,
the one Force which watches over all ya.

Stoppin all this hate from religion to religion,
that would end the DiscrimiNation,
and it would return us under any God to that one nation.
It would stop the crucifism of homosexualism
and put a halt to all the racism.
The way I see it we all live under the same roof,
learning to accept other religions
just may make all the world's problems go poof.
And then there would be Peace,
Freedom,
Acceptance,
and Love for All under this roof.

Temporary Closure on Fight #1

Peace brings freedom.
Freedom brings acceptance.
Acceptance brings love.
Love brings peace, freedom, and acceptance.

If we all learn to be in peace,
if we all learn to give the freedom we all deserve,
if we all learn to accept,
if we all learn to love,
we will be able to come together as one.

Hopefully we can see the importance of stopping hate.
Hopefully we can see the importance of holding Peace,
Freedom, Acceptance, and Love.
If we can't see it then I feel sorry for our soul.
And my fight over this subject isn't done.
Y'all can be sure I'ma battle this first fight till my life is done.

For now my fight moves onto one that still deals with hatred,
but also deals with issues more dangerous and much larger
than the hate I fought just now.
It's another fight that may be impossible to win,
but I'ma go after it anyway.
And of course,
I'ma do it through my poetry.

Here we go,
yet again...

Fight #2

*America and the World:
Expression, Opinion, Vision,
Rights, Betterment.*

Ty Brack

A Fight #2 Briefing

This is the fight where people from all walks of life
lock hands and forget about any differences we've
had,
in order to express our rights to express ourselves,
without bein sent on the Out of America Express.

This is where we fight for our right to say what we
like,
without it hurtin our chances of getting hired
over someone who has the same opinions as the boss
who decides who's hired.

This is where we fight for our right
to not be locked out of a party at night,
because of our opinions about a war,
even though the party has nothing to do with that war.

This is where we fight for our right to write what we
like
and what we believe without an offended person
or the government pullin a trick out their sleeve.
Because that's the kind of trick the First
Amendment's supposed to prevent from bein pulled
out anybody's sleeve.

        This is what this fight's all about.
          It's time to start Fight #2...

Banned, Restricted, and Censored

Teen angst, homosexuality, religious beliefs, and cussing.
These are some of the subjects that have left people fussing
over books which hold such content.
Books that offend certain people to an extent
to where they take it in their own hands,
to decide to devise devious plans,
that somehow find a way to get such books banned
from schools and bookstores thanks to their commands.

Only problem with this is such books
can actually have positive outlooks,
if they would just be given a chance to advance
without sufferin from someone's religious or political stance
that never allows these books to get to young reader's hands.

And it's too bad,
these books might just change young reader's thoughts.
That's why it's a shame
that such books with so many lessons to be taught
can just be hidden away and left to rot.
In addition to the fact,
this whole process is a violation of the freedom of press
the First Amendment is supposed to allow us to express.
Hell,
this book contains all those touchy subjects listed way

above.
I guess I'ma be the next author who'll be banned and a victim thereof.

Not only have books suffered,
music is constantly bein uncovered
for teachin the wrong messages to our youth,
when really all music does is present the truth,
about where an artist comes from
and the struggles that artist has overcome.
But some people take music too damn literally.
A lotta times what's bein said is bein said artistically,
so it doesn't mean what you think it means.
Like when Tupac Shakur talked about "Thug Life,"
people thought he was promotin the use of a gun and a knife.
He was really talkin of fightin through poverty stricken life.

And therein lies the problem,
some people want to ban music without really listenin.
Music is just expressin the artists' opinion
and all the shit they been involved in
so that their fans have someone to believe in
and someone in their life who's inspirin.
With the want to ban, censor, or restrict certain types of music we once again,
have another example of a violation
of a right the First Amendment is supposed to be providin.

Often it's not a matter of a song bein completely banned.
Often it's a matter of what time the song can be un-

canned.
Like when pro-war music videos play durin prime-time,
yet anti-war ones are played at three in the morning time.
Just sounds like one more instance
of the First Amendment bein shoved off in the distance.

The Founding Fathers never dreamed they'd be invented.
Television, movies, and the Internet got people all
demented.
Subliminal messages transmitted through these mediums,
parents and politicians constantly shout for regulations
from the government,
till they step in and force these mediums to concede to
them.

Ratings systems, advisory warnings, and special time
slots,
the First Amendment continues to get shot.
Whatever happened to "Congress shall make no law?"
These are communications the Founding Fathers never
saw,
but they still look on with an open-jaw.

The thought behind the First Amendment was,
the more opinions people express,
the more the truth should surface,
and the more hate would digress.
The Fathers figured people could figure this out
individually.
It's called bein an individual who's self-governing.
That's what America was based upon,
government that is limited and people who have freedom.
But the media bein banned, restricted, and censored,

that doesn't sound like limited government to me.
It sounds more like government take-over to me.
So if you don't like what ya read, hear, or see,
don't call out for Big Brother,
and have Big Brother take away the rights of another.
Let the author, musician, or director present their work.
Let them do it the way they originally intended for it to look.
Takin all that away is breakin the First Amendment,
takin all that away is actin like a crook.

The Right Idea

Before we move on, I just want to point out that lately there is a lot of talk of what is un-American and what is American, who is a traitor and who isn't a traitor to America. A lot of people think that if someone speaks out against something the government does, then that person is un-American and is therefore a traitor. But if you remember, the First Amendment gives anyone the right to say anything, so in reality they are American because they are just expressing their rights as given in the First Amendment.

Do you remember in the spring of 2003, when the Dixie Chicks' lead singer, Natalie Maines, said some intriguing comments about President Bush at a concert in England? Remember how people started smashing Dixie Chicks cd's after those comments were made and how country music radio stations basically banned the Chicks' music from being played? That's an example of this thought that people who speak out against the government are un-American and therefore traitors. The Dixie Chicks have the right to express their opinion or opinions. Sure, the people who smashed their cd's have the right to smash their cd's, but are the Chicks really un-American? No. They are American because they aren't afraid of standing up and using their First Amendment rights no matter what people will think. And should they be banned from radio stations? Probably not. The stations have the right to do so, but there are still Dixie Chicks fans out there who want to hear their music, and if other listeners don't like it, they can just change the station for three minutes of their life. Because believe it or not, there are people who don't think of the Dixie Chicks as un-American or as traitors. There are people out there who don't like what Natalie said, but still listen to the Chicks' music because those people understand she has the right to say what she wants. They understand that Natalie's beliefs about President Bush or the war doesn't change the Chicks' music to bad music. These are the people who have the right idea and these are the people who exemplify the definition of…

A True Patriot

A True Patriot…

is honest and dependable,
along with being an individual,
but cares and has love for others as well.

A True Patriot…

is not afraid to question leadership.
or are they afraid to lead themselves.
Nor are they afraid to make mistakes,
and be able to take responsibility for their mistakes.

A True Patriot...

Is not reluctant to criticize or defend their government.
And they are able to listen to the opinions of other patriots
without going to any extremes,
such as calling the opinions of other patriots un-patriotic.

A True Patriot...

Seeks the truth in order to find a better way.
A better way for themselves, their country, and the world.
They do this by understanding and fighting for their rights,
and by bringing other people up to fight with them.

Are you a True Patriot?

In the Dark

This one goes to those True Patriots livin in the dark.
Those True Patriots who don't know where to start.
Who've been betrayed by high school history books
cuz they gave them a false sense of how everything looks.

Then from high school the True Patriots graduate,
and learn our past and present is filled with lies and hate.
And it scares the True Patriots to think about it,
so they hide cuz they're confused on what to do about it.
Or they hide cuz it's all happenin far away,
so they may think it doesn't affect them on the day to day.
Trust me it affects us all in some way.
It doesn't have to be 9/11 to affect us in some way.
So here's what you True Patriots can do in addition to pray,
you can express your right to "a redress of grievances."
That means you can bitch about the government,
supposedly without sufferin any consequences.

So I'm tellin all of you,
the True Patriot lies within you.
And a True Patriot starts by askin to be given what's true…

Give Us the Truth

Take me to a land that doesn't exist,
take me to the place where the truth isn't just a wish,
a wish that not enough insist,
and if we do insist,
we'll more than likely end up being denied this wish.

Cuz if we want our government to come clean,
we can send in a request to the Machine.
It's called a Freedom of Information Request,
or F.O.I.
But believe it or not,
the Machine doesn't always comply.
It can take your request and stamp it with a *deny*.
I'm not sayin I've never lied.
Hell,
I think we all at some point tell a lie.
But our lies are shit like,
"I couldn't wash the dishes ma,
I had soap in my eye."
When the Machine lies,
it's about shit that could cause people to die.
The Machine'll say it's considered National Security.
And it says if we know the truth it could harm our security.
But if the truth really is National Security,
then don't we the people of the nation have the right to know the truth behind the threat to our security?

What the Machine does is try to protect us from the truth.

So if we're lucky they'll tell us half the truth.
The Machine will withhold important info,
cuz if we know the full truth,
the Machine thinks we'll panic and blow their roof.

So they continue to lie,
and they do so with a convincing look in their eye.
Politicians have Public Relations campaigns,
designed to make them look better and their opponent worse,
so they can win an election and pop bottles of champagne.
Then they get in office because of votes from you,
and do none of the shit their campaigns promised they'd do.

Let's see,
Vietnam could be won,
Nixon wasn't a crook,
Reagan knew nothing of the Contra and Cocaine connections,
Clinton only gave Monica a pleasant look,
and Bush's people didn't rig an election.
Just some examples of lies,
when later revealed to the public caused an up-rise.

If we'da been told the truth in the first place,
all this cynicism wouldn't be such common place.
But instead,
the Machine decided bein lied to was in our best interest.
Maybe that's why so many people have lost interest.
Maybe if they would give it to us straight,

no matter how un-settling the truth may at first taste,
people will regain trust and stop sayin the Prez is a waste.
Maybe then we young people will start castin our votes,
cuz insteada seein a buncha old goats,
we'll see candidates who speak to us,
and are worthy of a trip to the ballot box from us.
Maybe then we'll respect their decisions,
there won't be so many criticisms,
we won't go and blow the roof,
if they would just give us the truth.

Ty Brack

Vision of a President

Give me a President with numerous tattoos,
with a love for hip-hop, rock, rhythm and blues.

Give me a President who struggled through poverty,
who wasn't part of a rich family with tons of property,
who doesn't come from a wealthy political history,
and who doesn't keep past mistakes a mystery.

Give me a President who got high.
Who got drunk and slapped with a DUI,
but isn't afraid to look the public in the eye,
to tell them in the first place to avoid an outcry.
They'll admit,
"I was young and I was dumb,
we all make mistakes we learn from."

This is a President who seems closer,
who doesn't appear to be a poser.

This is a President who'll break the routine of old white men.
Maybe it'll be an African American,
or a Mexican,
or maybe even a Woman.

Whoever it is,
that person above,
is my vision of a President.

A Fight #2 Checkpoint

Bans, restrictions, censorship,
check.
True patriotism,
check.
Searching for truth,
check.
Vision for the presidency,
check.
Abortion rights,
…wait that's a different fight,
plus that's next book anyway.
Middle class bias toward poverty and extremely wealthy,
that's the next book too.
C'mon Fly think.
Stay focused on what's important right now.
What else is there to cover for this book and this fight?
Oh yeah, oh yeah.
I got it now.
I love this one.
Make sure you…

Support Your Troops!

"If you don't like it, then don't live here!"
"The least you can do is support your troops!"

Ty Brack

Of course I support.
Of course we support.
Just cuz we don't like a war don't mean we don't support.
Just cuz we don't like a war don't mean you can get us fired,
or make it impossible for us to get hired,
or hold us out of social functions,
like y'all did to Susan Sarandon and Tim Robbins,
when they were held out of a movie Hall of Fame induction.

We love America and our troops.
That's why we oppose the war in groups.
We have the right to assemble peaceably.
But protestors,
understand blockin freeway traffic isn't peaceful assembly.
In the eyes of others that gives all of us a hater rep.
That gives people the idea to label us with a traitor rep.
But belong to this rep all of us don't.
Should we accept this idea of a rep,
I won't.

I feel for all our service people.
Everyday I think about these people.
I'm nineteen.
My life is simple and serene.
They're nineteen.
Their lives aren't so simple and serene.
They're experiencing bullshit I could never dream.

And laws say they're old enough to fight with a
chance of never gettin their life back.
But when they get back,
laws say they're not old enough to go to a bar and
take a shot from Jack.

And I'm sure they're all countin down the days,
to when they get to come home and see their mom's
face.
I have friends who are overseas along with 'em,
as well as friends of friends to go along with them,
so I'm countin down the days along with 'em.
See I told you this affects us all somehow.
Of course I support our troops for cryin out loud.

Maybe it's the other way round.
Maybe if you're pro-war,
you don't support the troops in the air or on the
ground.
Cuz y'all so quick to judge,
so quick to give the nudge,
and send troops into war,
without thinkin bout what awaits them on the foreign
shore.

Now the shoe's on your foot
and it don't fit so good now does it?
So sayin we don't support the troops don't seem like
it was such a good idea then was it?

One last word before Fight #2 continues on some
more,
just know just cuz we don't support a current war

don't mean we won't support a future war.
It all lies within the cause we're given,
and the facts we are or aren't given
about how the proposed war will affect the world we
live in.
And in order to decide if you're for,
or against a war,
just ask yourselves…

Is It Worth It?

Release the demons,
unleash the hounds,
hear the sirens sound.
War is abound.
War is in our background.
War is in our foreground.

Helicopters crashing,
tanks thrashing,
news cameras flashing.
Children screaming,
soldiers bleeding,
the maximum limits of fear exceeding.
Are we succeeding?
The enemy or ourselves,
who are we defeating?

Poetry is Power

Saddam's been found.
Do we need to stick around?
Doesn't Bin Laden need to be killed?
Does the goal to find the weapons still need to be fulfilled?
Is there still oil to be drilled?
Have we fucked with free-will?

Iraq needed liberation you see.
America intervened to change them to democracy.
Who said they wanted to change completely.
Maybe they just needed help with Saddam to get free.
Maybe now they want left alone to create their own society,
one based on their own cultural originality.

Right-wingers are right.
Left-wingers are full of un-patriotic spite.
No one can agree.
Everyone argues just to disagree.
How can we fight in another country?
We're fighting ourselves in our own country.

87 billion.
There's shit in America that needs rebuildin.
Put some of that 87 billion toward a defense system.
A system that protects us and our freedom.
Other enemies are plottin and schemin.
They all have reasons to get even.
Shouldn't we be given them more attention?

Are we wastin our time?
Soldiers dyin everyday on the front line.

Ty Brack

And for what?
Should I keep my mouth shut?
Does it all need correcting?
What's the point of it all directly?
The main question,
let's unearth it.
Ask yourselves again,
is it worth it?

Our Future

This is the final stage in this current quest,
but before we lay it to a temporary rest,
I must say Saddam has gotten and will get what he's deserved,
and in that case justice has been and will be served.
Let me also say that I've decided the rest of it's not worth it,
cuz I looked to the future and its full of bullshit.

People have completely lost the ability to be self-governing,
Big Bro is constantly hovering,
and so many laws have been made that the Constitution is no longer able to be covering.

The few True Patriots who chose not to live in the dark,
tried for change and tried to light a spark,
but have been outcast and sentenced to life in that dark.

We've tried to help struggling countries,
but we did so with force.
And all that force,
just brought about more force,
and now life on Earth has nearly run it's course.

We're on the brink of nuclear war.
So many bad decisions made leadin to this point,
our only option is to join in World War III,

even though there's no point,
even though there's no possible way of savin the joint.

Everyone and everything is screwed.
One push of a button and all life will be removed.
But no one knows life's teetering on the edge.
No one has a clue,
we're all robots,
and we all believe the head Machine is tellin us what's true.
Except all we've been told is there's a war.
No mention of a nuclear war on the brink,
no mention of life seconds away from being extinct.
Just another one of those half-truths,
and there's nothing anyone can do,
cuz all the True Patriots are part of a prison crew.

Suddenly the button's been pushed,
nukes explodin everywhere,
Nuclear Winter fills the air.
Life that wasn't blown up durin the explodin
is slowly losin steam and erodin.
Everyone and everything is screwed.
A result of betraying ourselves,
and lettin ourselves be betrayed.
Now the once beautiful Earth is just left to decay.

I know it all sounds crazy,
but it's the craziest shit that usually happens.
At the rate we're going,
I wouldn't be surprised if in the future all that happens.

And I know it all sounds pretty fuckin depressing,
but that's why I want y'all to understand that you have the fuckin blessing,
of being able to fight in order to start a worldwide reconstruction,
and save us all from this current path of worldwide destruction.

Cept we must also put this fight on hold,
in order to continue it in the near future,
we must first find inspiration,
and a purpose we can hold.
We must move my poetry onto Part Four,
and figure out what it is we live for.

Part IV

What Are We Living For?

This may be a question you're asking yourself right now or you've asked yourself before. There's a lot that goes on in the world that can cause one to become depressed and lose their way. Everything I've expressed so far in the first three parts of the book is just part of what can cause someone to become depressed and lose their way. Often times for me, it's hard to think about all the problems outside of myself, along with the family, relationship, and sexuality problems that are within me, and still be able find a purpose to keep on existing.

I know most of you have felt this way too. I know my life compared to most, probably looks like a cake walk and you are probably having a harder time than me trying to figure out what to do with your life and if you have a reason. And that's what this final part, **Part IV**, is all about. **Part IV** is dedicated to all those who wonder why we're here? What we have in our lives to look forward to day in and day out? What inspires us to keep going? Who should we look to for inspiration? Who should we look to as our heroes? What can each of us individually do to help better the world? How can we use our poetry as power and what is our poetry?

Well, this is where we find out.
Here we go one more time…

Ty Brack

My Inspiration

I'm gonna to tell you where my inspiration comes from because your inspiration may come from the same places as mine. Or maybe reading about my inspiration will make you think about who and what inspires you and may give you a greater appreciation for the sources of your inspiration.

So, here is my inspiration...

There are many things that inspire me.
For instance,
books, music, and movies.
The wider the spectrum,
the more I learn,
and the more I yearn
to continue widening that spectrum.
Thanks to the likes of J.D. Salinger and Tim O'Brien.
Tupac Shakur and Eminem.
U2, Alicia Keys, and Gwen Stefani.
Oliver Stone, Peter Jackson, and Spike Lee.
Them and more taught me of how life's filled with oppression,
but they also helped me battle through times of depression.
And I think it's safe to say
we can all take something away
from what all of them have to say.

There's also the people in my life who are here for real.
The people who'll do anything for me,
look out for me,

and teach lessons to me.
My father, brother, and the rest of my friends and family,
even though they haven't always understood me.
Plus a man I call Sweetie,
a teacher I call Huff,
and what the hell,
I'd be lyin if I didn't say Haley McKell
inspired me as well.

But if there's one person most responsible for inspiring me,
one person most important to me,
it's the one person who's always encouraging,
with the ability to bring me back to reality.
It's the person who gave me desire durin a heart-to-heart
about this book and if I should even start.
All it took were four words said to me,
"You show 'em Ty."
Those four words set me free.
This person is my mother,
I love her.

Thank you all for inspiring me with your poetry.

Ty Brack

Real Heroes

(The people in this poem are based on real people and real situations and stories, but the names of these people are fictional.)

I know everybody has their pop-culture heroes, hell, I just told you some of mine. And I know everybody has friends and family who are their heroes as well, I just listed some of those too. Though these people do inspire us and are heroes in their own right, there are people who are real-life heroes who've been lost in the shuffle. They are people we forget while we're wrapped up in the television screen. These are the people who are the true fighters, true survivors, True Patriots, these are our Real Heroes…

He's just been brought into the world,
born months pre-mature.
If he'll live,
the doctors aren't sure.
His parents haven't even had time to decide on a name yet.
They decide to name him Michael,
but while that's bein set,
Michael's been put on life support.
The doctors come up with the report,
even if he lives through the initial experience,
he has defects that won't allow him to do things we experience,
like play a sport.

His parents look on from the outside,

both are torn up on the inside
cuz they know no one should have to go through
what their little boy is gonna have to.

Weeks pass and Michael's still fighting,
till one day there's finally a glimpse of bright lighting.
He can come home for the first time,
but the doctors still say he doesn't have much time.

So his parents cherish everyday that passes by,
in which they can still look him in his beautiful blue
eyes.
Michael cracks his first smile.
His parents break down and cry,
cuz they're so thankful he's still alive.
Cuz they know each beat of his little heart
contains more courage, bravery, and fight,
than any person could muster with all their might.

Michael is one of our real heroes.
Not the people you see on reality TV shows.

Alicia's sixteen,
pretty enough to be a beauty queen.
Cept she has no time for that.
She's got school, work, and her parents are divorced
and never available to talk at.

Oh yeah,
she's gonna be a teenage mom.
Thanks to some asshole named Tom.
Alicia thought it could never happen to her,
but she had no one to protect her.

She tried to escape,
but Tom pinned her down and it was too late.
She became a victim of rape.

Her child's gonna be a product of evil demon's semen,
but it's her choice and she knows her daughter has a reason.
So she chooses to keep her little girl,
cuz Alicia's parents were never there for her as a little girl.
Alicia was able to raise herself,
so she believes she can raise a little girl by herself.
Alicia knows every time she'll see her daughter laugh,
she'll be able to realize it's not all that bad,
she's determined to give her daughter the life she never had.

Alicia is gonna keep movin on,
even though everything that's happened to her causes a lotta hurtin,
she still goes to school and keeps workin,
she doesn't give in,
she keeps livin.

Alicia and Michael are two of our real heroes.
Not the people you see on political banter TV shows.

David just spent a year in Iraq.
That's a year of his life he's never gettin back.
He's glad to be home,
but he's got memories he doesn't wanna share over

                                              the phone,
                                            or in person,
                                           or with anyone,
                                      not even his own mom.

The only reason he joined is cuz he didn't know what
                                                  else to do.
Plus his father was pushin him into shit he didn't want
                                                      to do,
                  that's why he got on that plane and flew.
                  He had no idea of what he was gettin into.

                                                  While there,
                             David survived a helicopter crash.
He saw fellow soldiers go in and outta the death flash.
                                               Not to mention,
                    he accidentally killed an innocent citizen.
Now David's always gonna have that in backa his
                                                        mind.
Lately it seems to come to the front of his mind all the
                                                        time.
He's still only twenty and has his whole life aheada
                                                         him,
            but feels like the man he killed should be livin
                                                 insteada him.

                                                Despite all this,
        David knows suicide is the easy way to be leavin.
He can see that no matter what the people believe in,
     whether or not they think the cause is a justifiable
                                                      reason,
            that no matter what he was forced to do for our
                                                     freedom,

he is seen in everyone's eyes as a hero,
and that's enough to keep David breathin.

David, Alicia, and Michael are just some of our real heroes.
There are more people like them who fight through struggles everyday and are also our real heroes.
Unlike the fake people we see on TV shows.

To all you real heroes out there, God bless you. Keep fighting, keep finding, and keep using your poetry.

Moments

It's going to a movie that makes you cry,
enterin an art contest and winnin first prize,
passin a test in which fills you with pride,
or writin an entire book to everyone's surprise.

It's bein at a party with all your best friends,
your diploma at graduation,
goin to a concert for your favorite band,
bein part of thirty-thousand fans singin in unison.
Or startin your own band,
rockin a small stage for the first time,
with hardly anyone there to give you a hand.

It's the taste of your first kiss,
knowin it's the person you can spend eternity with,
makin meaningful love for the first time,
and doin it over and over still as if it were the first time.

It's the birth of your first and every child,
watchin them grow up and all the times they make you smile,
growin old with the person you knew was the one,
lookin them in the eye after fifty years,
and still knowin they're the one.

These are the moments we all live for.
These are just some examples,
I'm sure you can think of more.

These are the moments we all work hard for.
When they come along,
we cherish,
remember,
and then they pass on.
Then we go back to work,
until the next great moment comes along.

These are the moments that already have and soon will contribute to my poetry, your poetry, and everyone's poetry.

So What?

"So what Ty or Flyvek or whatever your name is. What good does it do me to know who our real heroes are or what moments we live for or where our inspiration comes from? I still don't know what my purpose and what I'm supposed to do. And what's this poetry we're supposed to find that you keep talking about?"

Well, I'll get to the poetry question soon enough. But first, if you're a person thinking like that, let me give you some words…

Of Encouragement and Advice

So,
ya don't know what to do with yourself,
all your ideas get shut down or put on a shelf.
Man,
fuck that,
don't flow with that,
don't fall victim to that,
stand up and fight that.

So,
you've been told by adults you're just young and ambitious,
and to not even try cuz you won't reach any of your wishes.
Man,
fuck that too,
but understand they're just tryin to protect you.
But understand this too,
young and ambitious is a great gift.
With this gift you have the time and energy to reach and lift.
You have the time and energy to explore all your ambitions,
and explore all your life intentions.

Go as many places as you will,
the more you will,
the more people you meet,
you will.
Each person will have a different story to tell,

with important lessons you can learn from as well.

Plus the more places you go,
the more you'll grow.
You'll go through shit that'll make a better person
outta you,
and prepare you for situations that lie aheada you.
Situations that before you know it will be apparent,
like becoming a parent.

That's why you should get up,
soak as much as you can up,
but don't be afraid to mess up,
cuz you most likely will,
we all do,
but when you do,
don't give up,
get back up,
keep soakin it all up,
eventually you'll find your niche and you'll live it up.

Just think bout how our generation
has the power to change the face of our ongoin
creation.
We can take all these problems we currently facin,
and we can eliminate em.
Cuz we are the future leaders of this world and this
nation.

And if part of the older generation
wants to fear our generation
cuz they're afraid of what we're gonna be,
then let em be.

They need to remember they were young once like you and me.
Like they never went to parties, got drunk or smoked weed.

It is this generation that will make a difference.
We can be peaceful,
have love for all people,
understand our rights and be expressful,
all while still bein accessible.
Insteada passin down misunderstandings, disbeliefs,
and orders just to show the youth our muscles can be flexed.
We can start a new tradition,
we can pass down encouragement from our generation
to the next.

This goes for all generations not just mine,
please don't figure all this out when you've run outta time.
And if y'all don't believe me,
if y'all think ya can't make a contribution to the change of the world's insanity,
all you have to do is branch away from the tree,
all you have to do is find your poetry.

Ty Brack

Poetry is Power

Webster's Revised Unabridged Dictionary defines poetry as, "Imaginative language or composition, whether expressed rhythmically or in prose."

That's the dictionary definition,
but here's the real definition.

Poetry is what is inside all of us.
And that poetry inside can be power if you find a way to express.
And if you express,
the way through which you express
becomes your poetry and your power.

Just so happens,
my writin, speakin, and poetry,
is my poetry.
That may be yours too,
but your poetry may be different than me.
You may have already found it,
may have never even thought about it,
just now realized it,
or are searching and are yet to find it.

If you have no clue as to what your poetry should be,
or could be,
don't quit and be satisfied with the boring-old flow,
you can get out there and enhance what you already know,
then through that knowledge you can set your goal.

Poetry is Power

Just to name a few for ya,
your poetry could be in the form of a teacher,
a preacher,
a waiter or waitress,
an actor or actress,
a coach,
a nurse,
a doctor,
a janitor,
or a gas-station manager.
Whatever it is you do,
if you use it to express what's in you,
and you do it to help others get through,
then it is your poetry and it is your power.

Maybe you have a clue of what you want your poetry
to be,
but you're stuck in a place that won't allow your
poetry to be all it can be.
If that's the case,
keep workin to get outta that place.
Take the advice of other people's poetry to heart,
soon enough you'll find a way for your poetry to start.
And while you're workin toward your poetry,
just remember,
you can use that place you're stuck in to begin
practicin,
your poetry and your power.

Ya see all this is what I mean by findin your poetry.
This is why I keep askin ya to think about your
poetry,
and whether or not you've found it yet.

Ty Brack

Cuz once you find it,
it's amazing how much good it can bring,
it's amazing how much it can make you feel like a queen or a king.

But make sure once you find it
that you don't try to deny it,
and please don't try to confine it.
And make sure you don't use your poetry as an excuse to hate,
cuz real poetry doesn't come outta that crate.

Just as long as it's true to what's inside,
as long as it's helpin others on the outside,
as long as you expand and learn from other's poetry,
as long as you use it with a harnessed tenacity,
which allows you to express purposefully and positively toward the continuing development of your society,
and as long as you use it till the day your body's died,
your soul will live on
and your poetry will live on in the hearts of those you touched while alive.

All because your poetry is your power.
All because ***Poetry is Power.***

Before We Close the Book

We must take a look back and then a look forward. First the look back, remember this book was not only written for me to keep my sanity and express myself, but it was written for all of you to find something you can relate to, help you through a tough time in your life, or open your eyes to something you never thought about before. I know it worked for me and I hope it worked for you as well.

If anything I said in this book offended you, I'm sorry, that was not my intention. I was not trying to run down my family, my first love, the government, or anyone else. I was simply releasing my thoughts, experiences, and beliefs in order to pass them onto others in hopes of bettering one person to the next. And by doing this, if I helped one person, if one idea struck a chord with just one person, then like I said in the beginning, my job has been done. My slight role in the changing the world has been played, and believe me, I'm going to continue to play it.

With that said, I have used my poetry to talk about myself and my inner struggles with my family, as well as relationships and sexuality. I let in you into my personal life in the first half of the book because I wanted you to be able find experiences I've been through that you could relate to. And by relating to an experience I had, hopefully it helped you get through that experience peacefully.

In the second half, I used my poetry to express concern for hatred still lingering in our world as well as other problems in our world. The reason for that being a number of things; the first being that I wanted to inspire you to do something about these issues if you feel the same way I do about the issues I discussed. The second reason being that if you knew nothing or very little about these issues, I wanted to give you some info and insight into them and get you thinking in a different light than you have ever thought before. And the third reason was that I wanted to try and change the views of even just one person who thinks in hateful ways toward race, religion, or homosexuality, or a person who sees it fit to misuse the First Amendment or call people traitors for speaking out against the government.

Now that I have used my poetry to address all those subjects and purposes, we can take that look forward I was talking about. You've read the book and I've asked you to find your poetry, the question is, will you? Will you find it, or once you close the book will you just forget about it? I hope you search for and find your poetry. I hope you do because we can all learn from each other's poetry, hell, I already have learned from a number of people's poetry, but I want to learn from more.

See, the reason I kept giving you hints as to what poetry is, kept asking you to think about your poetry, to find your poetry, before I even told you what poetry really is, is because I wanted you to have that thought in the back of your mind as you read through my poetry. As you read through the poetry I was passing onto you, some of you may have been able to figure what I meant by finding your poetry, some of you may have not, but I wanted you to be thinking about what poetry means to you and how you can use what I was telling you. Then I told you what poetry is, so that you can find yours, use yours, and pass it on to others.

Sometimes it's hard even once you've found your poetry to go out and use it. Sometimes you know what your calling in life is, but you don't know if it's worth the time and effort to fulfill that calling. I went through that with this book, I was unsure as to whether or not it was worth the strain to try and get it published. I didn't want to offend anyone I love by something that I said in the book that they may not have known about me, or may not have known that I believed in a certain way of thinking that they don't believe in. But in the end it came down to knowing that no matter what I say, the people who love me will and should understand and it shouldn't change the way they look at me. And, if I didn't go through with publishing the book, I wouldn't have been true to myself. I talk about this fact in the final poem that will bring the book to a close, that's coming up after a couple more paragraphs.

So, if you're second-guessing yourself about how you should use your poetry or if you even should use it, don't worry because it is normal to second-guess yourself. Just remember whatever you decide on doing should be true to your heart and your mind. If you do that, you will no doubt be able to find and use your poetry in a positive and selfless way.

One more thing before we get to the last poem, please pass on any thoughts of mine that hit home with you through your poetry because the person you pass your poetry to will pass theirs to someone else, and it will continue. Trust me; the world would be a better place if we all found our poetry and used it as our power.

Now, before I finish using my poetry (for now), before we close the book, here's that one last poem I was talking about that will bring the entire book to its conclusion.

Here we go,
      one last time…

Conclusion Poem

Ya know, it's funny, I had this whole book written,
but I wasn't sure if I should go further with it and get
it published. But then, I decided to go further, and
this decision took place…

At a Red Light

I pull up to a red light,
a young Latino mother crossin the street,
holdin her little girl comes into my sight.
The mother looks tired,
mired in poverty,
cuz in this DiscrimiNation it's still so hard for a
minority to succeed.

Her little girl,
she's blind to the ways of the world,
a picture of innocence,
an innocence that will soon burn out like the
incense,
the incense inside my soul that has burned out as I
sit here at this red light.
I shouldn't be sayin what I'm sayin,
it's not right.

I don't wanna hurt my family,
my first love,
or offend someone who inspired me.
What if all the rhymin is too much,

what if people say it sucks,
what if someone finds wrong in what I believe?
I should just throw the book away,
start over,
try again another day.

Tupac's blarin through my stereo,
he's sayin he's not gonna change the world,
but he'll spark the brain that will.
What if I'm that brain?
What if my words spark that brain?
I look back at the mother and daughter.
Ya know what?
My thoughts shouldn't be contained,
my own mother's words,
"You show em Ty,"
have remained in my brain.

Suddenly I realize,
the book's not just bout makin my family understand me,
or standin up for what I believe.
It's for real heroes like the mother and daughter,
it's to help them get through times when they get harder.
The book's for people goin through tough times in a relationship or with family at home.
It'll let them know someone else is goin through similar situations and they're not alone.
It's about finding equality and love for everyone,
no matter what the sexual preference, race, or religion.
It's about inspirin people to stand up for their rights,

to search for the truth,
and fight to make their world better right now and for the future youth.
It's about inspirin people to find the poetry within,
hopin they'll keep expandin,
and hopin they'll pass their poetry to others to continue the inspirin.
And if I find someone or something that proves anything I said wrong,
I'ma take my own advice and stay strong,
I'ma admit I was wrong,
use my poetry to speak or write about how I was wrong,
then keep marchin on.

Cuz it's important to express what I've got to say,
it's important to share with people in my own way.
This book,
my microphone,
it's all my power and my poetry,
it's all part of what makes me strong enough to stay,
it's all part of the role I've been given to play.

Now the incense in my soul begin burnin again,
the little girl hasn't yet lost her innocence,
but I'ma be there for her when she does lose it,
and I'ma help her when her world gets all confusin.

The light turns green and I move forward,
it was at that red light I decided to move this book forward.
Now the book's been published and it's in your hands,

I hope it helped you separate yourself from the crowd
that always sits in the stands.
There's only eight more lines left then y'all can close
the book cuz it's through.
But before you do,
ask yourselves one more time,
how can you use all this poetry that I passed onto
you?
What are you gonna do?
What will your poetry and your power be?
All that is now up to you.

About the Author

Ty Brack, a.k.a. Flyvek, will be attending the University of Oregon in the fall where he plans to major in Broadcast Journalism and minor in Creative Writing. He has done a number of professional broadcasting jobs already and will continue to pursue more jobs in the near future.

Now 20-years old, Mr. Brack also plans to keep working on his career as an author with a follow-up to *Poetry is Power* in the works as well as his first novel.

I Sincerely Thank You

This acknowledgment page is for the people I didn't thank in the poem, "My Inspiration." This page is for my instructors and fellow students from WAR class at Lower Columbia Community College. Thank you for opening my eyes, making me expand, making me think deeper, and making me understand and accept. But most of all, I thank you for making me realize how I can express myself in a way that helps others, and not just me. I told you all at the end of the class that I would write a book and get it published, and that's what I did. This book is here because of all of you. It is as much yours as it is mine and anyone else who reads it. So, to all of you let me just say, *I sincerely thank you.*

This page is also for everyone else at Lower Columbia Community College, Chemeketa Community College, as well as everyone else who has been a part of my life and has given me advice, guidance, and opportunities. So, to all of you let me just say, *I sincerely thank you.*

And finally, this page is for all the real-life situations I have encountered, or anyone else has encountered, that allow us all to pass on our own unique stories, visions, and messages. These are the situations that don't need facts, figures, graphs, or charts to prove a point – a point that so often comes back to one simple, but sometimes so very difficult a concept to conceive – and that concept is love.

This page is for those real-life situations that continue to teach us that love, and all that goes with love, is what is most important in our poetry, our power, and our lives. It is these real-life situations that I have already written about and will continue to write about. It is that simple message of love that will continue to drive me onward. So, to all those real-life situations I've already encountered, you've already encountered, and that we are yet to encounter that will continue to prove to us that love is the answer and the key to power and poetry, let me just say with all my love, *I sincerely thank you.*